Priscilla's Prayer

George and Linda B

All images are either the Author's or a composite of contributions from Pixabay. Pixabay is a Creative Commons source and all are Copyright free. Significant contributing Pixabay artists from whom most of the main characters and visuals were created: susannp4 (Priscilla, mushrooms and other characters), Majabel_Creaciones (Aunt Dora), pendleburyannette (the tiny white-headed bird man, Wanda and others), SilviaP Design (nymph warriors), Ractapopulous (nymph warriors), LOSTMIND (Dora's Victorian House), VinnyCiro (Victorian interior room), Lizdunbar (Cilla's brother), DeeDee51 (Dora's fiancé Cilla's father), Parker_West (yellowjackets), Jazella and garten-gg (luggage), Anaterate (Cilla's grandfather), 708943 (Cilla's Angel), sergeitokmakov (angel wings), Sergeitokmakov (chicken), AILes (hats), KaosShots (books), Bambo (glass of milk), alisia_chris_al (breakfast), cocoparisienne (wallpaper and room), Pezibear (calf in a field), maja7777 (lamb).

Note: In addition to the above contributions there could be other Pixabay pieces that were used; however, my photography, images and creative recombination's comprise the majority. On Pixabay my identification is GeorgeB2, where I have published over 2,000 images. My photos and images have been viewed over one million times and downloaded for copyright free use over one half million times.

ISBN (Paperback): 979-8-9884655-2-2
ISBN (Hardcover): 979-8-9878693-9-0
ISBN (eBook): 979-8-9878693-8-3

Priscilla arrived at her new home. It was beautiful. It was tall and large. Larger than anything she had ever seen before. The house was her Aunt Dora's home. Priscilla was six and just old enough to wander in the yard and investigate her surroundings without being under constant supervision. Her nickname was Cilla, and nothing got past her sharp and curious mind.

Animals, insects, flowers, trees, and anything that moved was her passion. Cilla could read well; her mother had taught her before she died a few months ago. Her mother passed suddenly from the flu along with her father and little brother. She had lived on a farm far into the country and had since been sent to live with her Aunt Dora.

Dora was Cilla's mom's younger and only sister. Dora was engaged to be married, and Cilla had become a big complication.

Cilla had vivid dreams and visions during the day as well as at night. She had many new friends at Dora's house; they were both imaginary and real. While she blended them all together as she played, Cilla knew which experiences she could discuss with Dora and which she could not.

Next week there was to be a large yard party where Dora was to entertain several of her sorority sisters and discuss the upcoming wedding. Cilla's grandfather had spent the last week sprucing up the yard and house for the event.

It had not been decided just where Cilla would live. However, it was believed it was not proper for her to live with her grandfather.

Dora's fiancé was a bachelor and lawyer she had met at her church two years ago. He was ten years older than she and was starting his own practice. He was moving out of his uncle's firm to start his own. He was most proper, and matched Dora in every manner and formality.

Cilla was an unexpected obligation and was not a welcomed ingredient of the new couple's dream of their future. Her aunt was pleasant but not affectionate or attentive.

Cilla was asked to play in the yard away from the preparations. Dora would occasionally check where she was to ensure she would remain at a distance, for which Cilla was more than happy to oblige.

Her rounds began in the flower garden in the backyard. There she found her friend, a plump thrush that was hunting for worms and insects. Cilla often wondered what it would be like to fly. It must be a freedom people could not understand.

As she surveyed her domain, Cilla discovered almost everyone could fly except her. That seemed so strange. Even the bugs had wings. She imagined in her mind that she too could soar into the sky.

Cilla often missed her little brother and parents. They were very happy on the farm. She had many animal friends there.

She missed them all. Priscilla often dreamed about them and had conversations with her brother. He told her all she had to do was ask and he would come visit her no matter where she was.

There was also a strange tiny man with wild white hair who often caught Cilla's eye when she would survey her kingdom. He would often yell at Cilla to get her attention.

He always had birds around him of all different types. They seemed to be attracted to him. Though she mostly ignored the tiny man, Cilla felt she would one day meet this person.

So, several days before her aunt's big picnic, Cilla got the courage to talk to the strange little man. He told her there was danger in her kingdom. He said the patrol bees and their nymph riders had discovered an arch enemy. This enemy lived underground in a cavern where they plotted to take control of the entire yard. They were many in number and very aggressive with dangerous weapons.

The nymph warriors fought many battles with this enemy almost on a daily basis.

Her grandfather and Dora were building a croquet court in the lawn near where the picnic would be held later in the week. While hammering in the stakes at each end of the court, with a mallet, Cilla's grandfather accidentally unleashed chaos.

With each strike of the mallet, he caused vibrations in the underground nest. The angry insects came up from underground and attacked both Cilla's grandfather and her Aunt Dora who was standing nearby.

Both were stung many times and ran screaming for the house. Cilla was in the backyard and heard the commotion. She ran to see her family attacked by a swarm of angry insects but dared not get too close. Her grandfather yelled for her to go around the house and enter through the front door.

Cilla went to her room and began reading. She fell asleep and dreamed about making candy with her mother. Her father came in and noticed they were using peppermint oil to flavor the sweets. He said yellowjackets hate the same peppermint oil the two of them were using to make the candy and that he used the oil mixed with soapy water to run the pests away from nesting near the house and barn. So Priscilla had the solution to save Aunt Dora's party, peppermint oil mixed with soapy water!

The next morning Dora was very upset and worried about all the planning and efforts made for the party, that now had to be changed, and moved inside.

Cilla said, "When my mom and I made rock candy we used peppermint oil to flavor it. Daddy said the oil was good to shoo away yellowjackets. So, maybe we can use some to keep the pests away from your party."

Dora usually ignored Priscilla, but instead listened.

With an inquisitive and desperate look Dora responded, "Well, lets talk to your grandfather about that."

Soon, Dora, Priscilla, and Dora's grandfather were meeting. Grandfather Smyth listened intently to Cilla's story about her father using candy flavoring to repel their insect enemies and said, "An interesting concept but how did your father use the peppermint oil?"

Cilla stated with authority, "He put the oil in soapy water and poured the mixture through a funnel into the ground."

He responded, "Hmmm... sounds reasonable, problem is we don't know where the nests are."

Cilla then replied, "Give me a few days and I think I can show you where they come and go underground."

With an amazed look on their faces, Dora and her Grandfather nodded their heads and said, "Okay, as long as you are safe, don't go near the nests."

Gleefully, Priscilla ran out of the kitchen into the yard avoiding the area where the croquet court was set up. She quickly went to find the little man with the wild white hair. Within minutes, she talked to the plump thrush. The bird told Cilla the man was over at the old hickory stump, where he held flight school for some new bird riders.

She talked to the tiny man. He told her she needed to fly to talk to the Backyard Boss. She needed to fly there because his office was near the top of the huge oak tree on the property line in the rear of the backyard.

Priscilla asked, "Can you teach me to fly? I am running out of time to get things done!"

The man waved his hand and Cilla shrunk to one-one-hundredth of her normal size.
To her amazement, she became so tiny she could ride on the back of a bird.

After a few times getting on and off the bird's back, Cilla asked the bird to fly
her to the yard boss in the tall oak tree. Without a moment's delay they were off
the ground and flying. What a wonderful experience, Cilla was now flying like she
dreamed.

When Cilla landed in the enormous old tree, there was the Boss, a huge gray squirrel. He had his arms crossed setting on his limb, looking like a king.

She swallowed real deep and said; "Sir Boss, the yard has a problem, the yellowjackets are nested under the lawn and are about to take over your entire empire. With your help, I can remove these evil insects from your territory and keep them from coming back."

Sir Boss responded in a deep voice, "Well my little one, you are taking on quite a challenge, all of our bee and nymph riders are unable to defeat the yellowjackets. Do you think you can do what my army is unable to accomplish? What do you need from me?"

Cilla asserted, "I need to find the entrances and exits of their underground homes. I can then have the adult humans do the rest."

The regal squirrel said, "I will send you to my bee rider captain; her name is Wanda. She will get the information you want. I wish you and the humans great success."

Cilla flew her bird to Wanda's headquarters.

Priscilla told Wanda of her meeting with Sir Boss and what she needed. Wanda promised her army of bee riders would spy on the enemy and find their nests, but did not know how to mark their location so the humans could use their peppermint oil to drive the yellowjackets away.

Wanda set out with her best lieutenant. To get the information she needed, the courageous leader had to get very close to the enemy. This was a most danger-ous act and required great skill. They waited until it was almost dark. When night fell, however, they could fly no more and had to stay where they landed. You see, Wanda's bee mounts, as well as the enemy yellowjackets, need the sun's location and sunlight to locate landmarks so they can come and go without getting lost. Thus, flying at night was impossible for both bees and yellowjackets. Cilla had been told this by Wanda before she left to return home.

Dora was determined to marry, her fiancé, Smithfield. By any measure he was a good catch: successful, wealthy for his age, respectable and from a fine family. What else could she ask for? Her older sister, Margret, had chosen poorly and ended up dying on a small farm along with her husband, Ted and young son, William. Not only that, but she also left for Dora, her six-year-old daughter, Priscilla. What a horrible dilemma, what was she going to do with the girl?

Smithfield, ten years her senior, felt much like Dora. Priscilla was a problem, based both on Dora's happiness and his plans for a family.

Grandfather Smyth had not bonded with Priscilla. He had only seen her once before her parents' untimely deaths. Now her unexpected reappearance was more of an imposition than a blessing to his busy and full life.

Cilla was dreaming about flying and the battle with the evil insects when her brother came to talk.

She was very glad to see him, and they talked about the upcoming events. He asked her how were the Bee Riders going to mark the yellowjacket's underground lairs? It had to be so visible their grandfather could find them easily. And to be safe, their grandad could only approach them in the dark hours. No doubt, if he acted during the day they would swarm out of their nest and attack him. Thus, the markings had to be something he could see at night.

Priscilla knew she had to talk to Wanda. There had to be a way to accomplish the marking. They were running out of time.

Dora and her father had a private discussion about Cilla.

Cilla's grandfather stated, "I don't think we should encourage the girl's fantasy about her taking care of the yellowjacket's. Doing so will make her imaginary world even more of a problem."

Dora thoughtfully responded, "I agree, however, if she can somehow help get rid of those infernal pests, I am willing to go along for a couple of days."

He relented, "If that is what you want dear, I will play along. But remember I warned you; it could make her worse. How can this little girl know how to deal with a threat adults are not able to manage? I recommend you simply move your entire party indoors and forget about the picnic and croquet tournament."

Cilla found Wanda and told her that Grandfather Smyth needed to fight the enemy at night. So, the entrance markings had to be visible to him.

Cilla suggested, "My brother and I talked about this in a dream, and we have a couple of suggestions. One is to somehow use fireflies to illuminate the openings. The other suggestion is to use foxfire. I located the fungus growing in the rotting interior of the old hickory tree stump."

Wanda thoughtfully responded, "We don't have time to persuade the fireflies to cooperate, so I think we are left with moving enough foxfire from the stump to the openings. I will get our bee riders to move as much as they can, as close as they can, near dusk this evening. We will have to move the fungus the rest of the way by hand after dark and place it to illuminate the openings."

Priscilla enthusiastically responded, "Thank you! I will tell Grandfather Smyth to look for the glowing rings in the lawn tonight after dark."

Cilla went to her grandfather's study. The room was still in Dora's home, where it would remain after he retired. Professor Smyth planned to give his prized library to Dora and her new husband. Cilla was fascinated by all the books and the high shelves going from the floor to within inches of the fifteen-foot-high ceiling. Cilla was not usually allowed in his study because, when there, he was doing research and preparing lectures and did not want to be distracted.

Priscilla reluctantly knocked on the door. She heard a gruff response, "Who is it?"

She said in a loud voice, "It is me, Cilla!"

"Well, come in and be quick about it, I am in the middle of some important preparations!"

Priscilla cracked the door just enough to slide in sideways and walked into the middle of the huge room and stood in front of her grandfather's massive desk. He put a book aside and looked down at her with his spectacles slid to almost the tip of his nose.

"Well, what do you want young lady?"

She said very respectfully, "Grandfather Smyth, preparations have been made to mark the entrances and exits of the yellowjacket's nests found within the croquet court. After dark tonight you may approach them without fear of being attacked because yellowjackets will not fly at night. The illuminated circles surrounding the holes are foxfire, a fungus that glows in the dark. You can then insert a funnel into the holes and pour the soapy water containing the peppermint oil."

"You didn't go near those holes, did you?"

"No sir! I promised you and Dora I would not!"

"Ok, I will play your silly game, because I promised Dora I would. However, when this fails, I hope you will learn an important lesson and stop living in your imaginary world."

"Yes, Grandfather Smyth, may I go now?"

"Yes, please! Close the door behind you!"

Wanda did as she promised, before dark she delivered the glowing fungus to be placed around the entrances and exits of the enemy.

That night, two hours after dark, Dora with her father went out to look at the croquet court. Dora's father protested at the waste of their efforts but went anyway. At first their eyes were adjusting to the dark as they had just left the lights in the house, and they saw nothing.

Professor Smyth grumbled again, "Just as I thought, nothing to see. I can't believe you made me carry this funnel and this five-gallon jug containing the oil and soapy water."

About that time Dora was about to agree, however, she just caught something glowing in the grass. It was faint but became more visible as she concentrated on them. She pointed them out to her father and after several moments he too was able to see them.

They approached with caution, not believing the beasts would not attack at night. One at a time, he inserted the funnel, and poured one third of the contents in each hole. With this done, they went in the house determined to test the results of their efforts the next day. Both Dora and her father were silent, not knowing what to say. They both slept poorly that night.

That night Cilla said her prayers and asked God for a miracle. In reading her Bible she remembered Daniel in the Lion's Den, the parting of the Red Sea, and others, would it be too much to ask for just one more?

She slept soundly and rose at sunrise. As was her new custom she got dressed and went to the kitchen to cook some oatmeal for breakfast. This morning, however, Dora was unexpectedly preparing the first meal of the day.

Dora, saw her and asked, "Priscilla, what can I make you for breakfast?"

Surprised, Cilla responded, "Oh, oatmeal is fine."

Dora suggested instead, "I think we can do better than that, how about bacon, eggs, and biscuits?"

Cilla said, "Yes, thank you Aunt Dora." *Thinking all along that God must have done that miracle she asked for last night.*

Her aunt told her to go into the dining room and sit at the table. When she entered the ornate room, her grandfather was there reading the newspaper. He pulled the paper down just enough to acknowledge her. She sat in one of the chairs opposite the professor.

Her grandfather, still reading, cleared his throat and said, "Seems those yellowjackets are gone this morning. Your Aunt Dora is very pleased. I don't know how this happened but however or whatever helped accomplish this is in my debt. What can you tell me?"

Priscilla said, "I know you and Aunt Dora think I am imagining things. But I can tell my imaginary world from the real world; however, sometimes the two overlap and a miracle is the result. I do not question everything; I hope you and Aunt Dora can do the same."

The professor dropped his paper, stared at Priscilla, smiled broadly, and said, "I must honor your statement, because I cannot refute your logic. Your reasoning is sound. I extend my apologies. Please accept both Aunt Dora's and my formal regrets for doubting you. We appreciate your courage and determination to help save the day for Dora's long anticipated festivities. Aunt Dora has requested your presence at her party today. Will you attend?

Cilla responded, "I would love to, but have nothing to wear to such a gathering."

He immediately and loudly said, "Well, we can fix that! Aunt Dora and I are taking you to the dress store as soon as it opens this morning. Would you like to go?"

Cilla eyes broadened and she almost laughed with joy, "Yes! Of course!"

The END